Signs of His Glory

Signs of His Glory

Some
Reflections
on
Miracles
in the
Gospels

Ronald Lunt

The Pentland Press
Edinburgh • Cambridge • Durham • USA

© Ronald Lunt 1997

First published in 1997 by
The Pentland Press Ltd.
1 Hutton Close
South Church
Bishop Auckland
Durham

All rights reserved.
Unauthorised duplication
contravenes existing laws.

British Library Cataloguing in Publication Data.
A catalogue record for this book is available
from the British Library.

ISBN 1 85821 533 1

Typeset by George Wishart & Associates, Whitley Bay.
Printed and bound by Antony Rowe Ltd., Chippenham.

*Dedicated to
my dear wife Mary*

CONTENTS

FOREWORD by The Right Reverend
Michael Langrish, Bishop of Birkenhead ix

INTRODUCTION
'I won't say it's a miracle ...' 1

I   SIGNS OF HIS GLORY
Miracles in the Gospels 5

II   THE LORD OF WHOLENESS
Miracles of Healing 17

III   THE LORD OF THE PRACTICAL
Miracles of Food and Drink 29

IV   THE LORD OF CREATION
Miracles of the Natural Elements 41

V   THE LORD OF LIFE
Miracles of Resurrection 53

FOREWORD

Coming out of the personal experience of a busy parish priest finding himself suddenly facing desperate illness through cancer of the spine, these reflections on our Lord's miracles offer not only a testimony to the reality of one man's faith and its strengthening, but a real encouragement to the faith of others. In *Signs of His Glory* Ronald Lunt guides us through the gospels to see the power of God at work in our own lives, and the life of the world around us.

Rooted as they are in the deep pastoral wisdom distilled from many years of practical parish ministry these Lenten meditations offer clear insights into the nature of prayer, and helpful encouragement to all concerned with people, their well-being and their care. In a fresh exploration of twelve different miracle stories this little book provides both an aid to personal devotion and also signs of hope for those who, like the author himself, find themselves facing one of life's crises or pains.

✠ Michael Birkenhead
February 1997

INTRODUCTION
'I won't say it's a miracle...'

This little book is based on a series of addresses which I gave during Lent 1996. Almost twelve months before that, I had been rushed into hospital, where cancer was diagnosed and it seemed doubtful whether I would ever walk again, or for that matter, even live for more than a few weeks. In fact, the turn around was quite amazing. After five weeks in three different hospitals, served by a team of doctors, nurses and physio-therapists, and a convalescence at home, I was in due course able to resume light duties. I gradually got back into full harness, resuming my rectorial duties for several months before starting an increasingly active retirement. Four months after I had been admitted to hospital, it was with great joy and thankfulness that I was able to preside over the Sunday Eucharist, which I had thought I would never do again.

During one consultation, a doctor of considerable reputation in the treatment of cancer came out with what was really just a throw-away remark, 'I won't say it's a *miracle*, but ...'. It was of course simply one of those off the cuff remarks in conversation, commenting on the fact that the treatment of my cancer had met with greater progress than was usual or was to be expected; but my immediate reaction was to think, 'Why not?' As I said at the time, it seemed to me that there were three factors which contributed to my progress. They were: the skill and dedication of doctors and nurses (which I will always remember with huge gratitude); my own faith and determination, and co-operation with what was being done for me; and the power of God at work in the situation, undergirded by an enormous volume of prayer in many different places involving literally many thousands of people.

Whether what has happened in my life is miraculous is not for me to judge. People have used the word miracle to describe the turn around in my condition; but then the word miracle is often used loosely in general conversation, or even used in television advertisements to describe the effects of washing powders! What I *am* certain of is that God's hand was very firmly on the tiller at that time, controlling the course of things in surprising and unexpected ways. I am not of course cured – I realise that my cancer is simply reduced and under control, and that I will no doubt need treatment and medication for the rest of my life – but the whole experience has greatly changed my life, and my perception of life.

It was that experience that got me thinking afresh about miracles, and how they are so often regarded (or, indeed, how loosely the term miracle is often used). At worst, they are regarded as a combination of circumstances, or quite ordinary explicable events that were seen as miracles by impressionable and imaginative minds. Looking at the miracles recorded in the Gospels, people will suggest natural explanations; for instance that at the Feeding of the Multitude, recorded in one form or another in all four Gospels, many of the crowd had picnics with them, which they brought out and shared at the appropriate moment – that the boy with the loaves and fishes was one of many who had come so prepared. Again, at the Miraculous Catch of fish where there had been none all night, it will be suggested that it was just a coincidence that there was a great movement of fish at the right moment; that with healings, it was just a state of mind, it was psychological . . . and so on. Or at best it is said that miracles are a thing of the past: they just don't happen any more; they are out of date, the environment isn't right for them. My own experience confirms for me that neither of those approaches to miracles will do. I am convinced that some remarkable things have happened in my own life, which have affected the course of things in surprising ways, not simply in the diagnosis and treatment of my illness, but in my spiritual pilgrimage, and that God's hand has been firmly on that development. I am equally convinced that that is often the case when God is brought into a situation: he often acts powerfully in ways that surprise us.

That was my starting point when I began to think about a series of addresses on Miracles and the Power of Prayer, looking afresh at some of the miracles recorded in the Gospels, and relating them to our own experience and situation, and to my own experience of illness, healing and wholeness. This little book doesn't claim to be a work of biblical exegesis, or of the theology of miracles. In the Gospels, there are many different miracles in many different situations, and it will only be possible to look at a few of them. Miracles are a huge subject; and I can only scratch the surface in a book of this size. However, my purpose here is not academic, but devotional. The incidents in the Gospels are not passed down to us to be of purely academic interest, but because of their significance for us now, in our own pilgrimage of faith.

Of course, miracles can present us with unanswerable problems. Why are certain situations, certain individuals, singled out for the amazing effect of divine intervention? For every Gospel situation to which the Lord brought an extraordinary turn around, there must have been many more where he was not encountered, and there was no miracle. This applies to our own experience too. Why does something amazing happen one time and not another? It's a question that goes through our minds in many tragic situations. Why does God allow it to happen? All too often, we can't answer that question: we are bewildered. In hospital, when we first knew of my initial diagnosis and the likely prognosis, my wife and I cried in one another's arms as we started to come to terms with the possibility of my imminent death; but that clearly was not yet God's will. I can only think that he had further work for me to do, and that I still had in some way purposes to fulfil to his glory. I hope among other things that in some way I might have been used to give encouragement to quite a number of people with chronic or terminal illnesses or facing major crises in life.

Certainly these things have greatly added to the richness of my life experience and of my spiritual pilgrimage; and I hope that in looking at some of the miracles in the Gospels in the light of that experience, these pages might be helpful to others.

I
SIGNS OF HIS GLORY
Miracles in the Gospels

'We beheld his glory'
(John 1, v. 14)

The miracles we read about in the Gospels are very varied, responding to quite different kinds of situations, and having effects in different areas of creation. We will be looking at a cross section of these incidents, and their significance for us. There are four major types of miracle in the Gospels, meeting four quite different kinds of need.

The largest category of course are the miracles of Healing – the turning around in a surprising way of some situation of illness that seems quite hopeless up to that point. There are situations where the diagnosis is wrong, or where there is no known way of dealing with the condition, where all the known ways have been tried and proved fruitless, or where the prognosis is hopeless. There are healings of cripples, of blindness, deafness and dumbness, of mental illness, of leprosy, of paralysis, of haemorrhage; a great variety of occasions where seemingly hopeless situations are amazingly transformed by the Lord's action.

Then there are miracles of Food and Drink, responding to

situations of embarrassment and inconvenience, such as the Feeding of the Multitude, which appears in various forms in the Gospels (Mark 6, vv. 35–44, Matthew 14, vv. 15-21, Luke 9, vv. 12–17 and John 6, vv. 1–14); the Turning of the Water into Wine at Cana in Galilee (John 2, vv. 1–11); and the Miraculous Catch of fish (Luke 5, vv. 4–11). Again, situations are changed dramatically and amazingly each time.

Then there are miracles involving the Elements: such as the Calming of the Storm (Mark 4, vv. 35–41, Matthew 8, vv. 23–27 and Luke 8, vv. 22–25); the Walking on the Water (Mark 6, vv. 45–52 and Matthew 14, vv. 22–33); and the Transfiguration (Mark 9, vv. 2–9, Matthew 17, vv. 1–9 and Luke 9, vv. 28–36). Again, they are all incidents which would never have been expected, events which run quite counter to the normal way of things.

The fourth type of miracle we find in the Gospels concerns Death and Resurrection: the Raising of Lazarus (John 11, vv. 32–45), the Raising of the widow's son at Nain (Luke 7, vv. 11–17), the Raising of Jairus's daughter (Mark 5 Matthew 9 and Luke 8), and of course the great climax of all four Gospels, the Resurrection of JESUS CHRIST HIMSELF. The Resurrection has to be seen as the greatest of all miracles, which totally turns everything around in so many ways – which is to Christians the watershed of history.

Varied as these different Gospel miracles are, six main strands are to be found running through them all, which say important things to us about life, and the powerful presence and action of God through it.

First, there is always **need** – weakness, helplessness. It's there in so many different situations: the desperation of a man blind from birth; of lepers with no hope of a cure, in pain and ostracised by everyone; of a man who was crippled and couldn't get near the healing waters of the pool of Bethesda, always being beaten to it by someone quicker off the mark; of the paralytic whose friends broke up the roof to let him down on a stretcher, in order to get him nearer to Jesus when the doorway was blocked by the crowds . . . and many other similar plights. Then there was the helplessness and embarrassment of those responsible for a wedding reception that had run out of wine; the crowds of hungry people with only scraps to feed them; the frustration of the fishermen who had toiled all night and caught nothing. There was the terror of the men in a tiny boat in a great storm at sea, in danger of being smashed to pieces like a matchbox; the despair of the sisters of Lazarus or the widow at Nain, or for that matter, the disciples themselves in the days following the Crucifixion. In such cases, there is a need, a weakness there, that no one can do anything about or cope with.

And when you have been desperately ill and totally dependent, as I have been, you've *been there*. In a sense, you identify with those people in those situations in the Gospels. It's one of the best ways I know of being reminded forcefully that we are not in control – GOD is. It was certainly a lesson I needed to learn personally. As a busy parish priest, I was involved in many areas of Church and secular life, from parish to General Synod and from charity work to civic relations, governorship of schools, etc, and I had tended, contrary to my own teaching over many years, to act as if *I* was in control of things, rushing here and there, 'keeping the show on the road'. The day I was rushed into hospital, I had to recognise that I wasn't indispensable, to let go of things and recognise that *He* was in control. It's a valuable lesson to grasp, in a world in which men and women increasingly think that with the technology at their disposal, they can engineer anything. In the Gospel incidents we will be looking at, we see first of all people in weakness and need coming to the Lord, fully aware of their helplessness.

Hand in hand with that weakness and need goes a particular kind of **humility**: the humility of recognising that you are totally dependent and that you are totally unable to escape by your own effort and will power. Humility is demonstrated time and time again in these Gospel incidents. A Roman centurion comes to Jesus, not demanding, in the manner of one used to giving orders, or from a position of lofty social superiority as a representative of the imperial power of Rome, but begging. He even says that he isn't worthy that Jesus should come under his roof. Lepers stand at a distance, pleading with Jesus to help them. People are dependent on others to bring them to him on stretchers. A blind man allows clay made with soil and spittle to be smeared over his eyes, and then depends on others to lead him through the city to wash in the pool of Siloam. A woman seeking the healing of her daughter accepts the humiliation of seeming to be brushed aside because she is of the wrong race (she is a Syro-Phoenician), and speaks of grovelling under the table to pick up the left over scraps. It goes on and on. There is no standing on dignity; there is deep humility, arising from need.

Again, I know from personal experience what it means to be totally dependent on others, in a way that means you can't stand on dignity; having to call a nurse simply to turn you over in bed, and to deal with your basic toiletries and feeding. I remember vividly being so embarrassed and apologetic when I had to call nurses for the third time to change the bedclothes because of the sudden effect of the medication I was on. Even much later on, as I convalesced and then started doing things again, there was the dependence on others in so many ways. It all gave me a glimpse of what it must be like to be in that kind of condition over a very long period, or even indefinitely. Above all, it means being brought forcefully to acknowledge that you are in God's hands, and in the hands of those whose skills, energies and commitment he is using. Being in that situation does a lot for creating the grace of humility and conquering pride. And that kind of humility – an acceptance of the indignity of total dependence – is where all the Gospel miracles begin, and where our Christian spiritual pilgrimage must begin too.

The third strand running through all the Gospel miracles, and the most vital of all, is the involvement of **Jesus Christ**. Time and time again it happens: hopeless cases of leprosy, paralysis, blindness, mental illness and so on change dramatically when *he* is brought into a situation. In the storm, when the little boat is being tossed about by the waves and the wind, and Jesus is asleep in the boat, the disciples wake him up, pleading, 'Save us, Lord; we perish'; and a word from him calms the storm. Peter, when he sees Jesus walking on the water, incredibly, steps out of the boat and walks on the waves towards him. It is only when he takes his eyes off Jesus and, looking down instead at the swirling waves, thinks in practical terms about the extraordinary, mad, stupid thing that he's doing, that he sinks and starts drowning. At the turning of water into wine at Cana, Mary brings the problem to Jesus – 'They have no wine' – and immediately the whole situation is transformed. If it had not been for the involvement of the Lord, no one would have dreamt of the outrageous step of filling the water pots with water and serving that to the guests (or, for that matter, attempting to feed five thousand people on five little loaves and a couple of fish, or attempting to catch fish where there had been no catch all night). As for the raising of the dead: it all seemed so unlikely, so impossible, until Jesus was brought into things.

Again, I've been there. The prayers, the anointing, the laying on of hands, the daily Communion that dedicated colleagues made possible for me, being able to read the Bible and the daily offices of Mattins and Evensong, these were at the heart of my hospitalisation weeks. I experienced a time of great weakness, of coming to terms with the serious nature of my illness and the possibility of imminent death; of changing diagnosis and uncertainty as to how active I would ever be again, of intensive treatment, and the long, slow weeks of making gradual progress, with all the frustration involved. Through all of that, everything was transformed because **CHRIST** was at the centre of it all – sacramentally and through the Scriptures – so that both the Eucharist and the Bible became even deeper and more meaningful truths for me than they already were. And that's so often the case. When he's at the centre of things, amazing things can happen – not just twenty centuries ago, but here and now. We need to be aware of his presence in quite down to earth situations – when walking down the street, or driving the car, when chained to the computer, the cooker or the sink, as well as the great moments of joy or sorrow, of pain or uncertainty – because that's the kind of God he is. Every facet of our lives is important to him, and his power and grace can transform every situation.

Side by side with that – an integral part of it of course – is **faith**. Quite amazing faith is so often encountered in the miracles recorded in the Gospels. In fact, Our Lord often remarks on the faith displayed: 'I have not found such great faith'; 'Your faith has made you whole'; and so on. It is the kind of faith that persuaded a blind man to allow himself to be guided through the busy streets of Jerusalem to wash off the clay in the pool of Siloam (John 9), or ten lepers to set off to the priests to seek a clean bill of health before they'd actually been healed (Luke 17), or a woman with a haemorrhage to touch the Lord's garment in the certain belief that by doing so she would be healed (Luke 8). It's the kind of faith that was involved when Peter stepped out onto the water to walk towards Jesus (Matthew 14); or when the disciples distributed what would, in our terms, be little more than five tea cakes and a couple of sardines to feed five thousand people. We could go on and on: there are countless instances in the Gospels of quite stupendous faith, which in terms of logic would seem quite crazy. And then of course, there's that great crowning miracle of the Resurrection, and the extraordinary change that came over the disciples and their approach to life as a result of the Resurrection experience. In none of these instances, of course, was the miracle itself the product of faith. When the Lord says, 'Your faith has saved you' or 'your faith has made you whole', he doesn't mean that the recipient has in any way created the miracle by an act of faith. What he does mean is that without the receptiveness of faith, they could not have benefited from the amazing and powerful act of God.

And that is so often true. Again, I know that faith played a major part in the facing of my own illness, and in the turn around in my condition that took place – not just my faith, but the faith of countless people who prayed for me throughout those days, weeks and months. In that situation, for all the activity and technology surrounding you, you are in many ways very much alone with God – silently conversing with him when you are alone in the scanner, or laid out in splendid isolation under the radio therapy machine, is a very special one-to-one experience. For me, those moments brought a quite fresh dimension to the meaning of prayer;

but it was the breadth of prayer support that so often overwhelmed me. What caused me literally to cry in my hospital bed was becoming aware of how wide and how full of faith was the net of prayer, as I received message after message, 'We are praying for you'; 'Our church is praying for you'. The messages came from many individuals and many churches, scattered all over the country and all over the world. I was told of candles lit at the Shrine of Our Lady of Walsingham; I was assured of prayers in places as widely scattered as Brazil and Melanesia. I became aware in a very real way of how wide, how vast and how varied was the Christian web of prayer. While I was in hospital having radiotherapy treatment, a long arranged Confirmation was taking place in my parish in Chester. That day, the Suffragan Bishop very thoughtfully came to the hospital to give me Holy Communion a couple of hours or so before he was due to officiate at the Confirmation, and promised to take my greetings to the candidates. At the time of the Confirmation, I was praying for the candidates, including those I had prepared; and they were praying for me. The next day, after the visitors had gone, I listened to the recording of the service they had made and brought to the hospital for me; and I was overwhelmed to the point of tears by the oneness we had in the powerful prayer of faith. That sense has never left me since. I was being made aware in a dramatic way of something that is always true. God is at work in many different situations, enabling people to come through very difficult phases in life, often bringing about surprising and amazing results; and prayer can be a powerful instrument in all that. It's important that we have faith. The answer to prayer isn't always what we are asking for or expecting; but God will always respond powerfully.

The fifth strand in the Gospel miracles is **action**. Very often

Signs of His Glory

in these incidents, Jesus requires people to *do* something, as the vehicle of what *he* is going to do. A cripple is told to pick up his stretcher and walk; a blind man is told to go and wash in a pool on the other side of the city; lepers are told to go and show themselves to the priests; fishermen are told to take their boats out again and cast their nets; waiters at a wedding reception are told to fill the water pots with water, and serve it to the guests as wine . . . and many other things. Often they are quite amazing things, quite ridiculous things when looked at logically – actions which require a great deal of faith.

That in itself is saying two important things. One is that these miracles happen not so that the recipients of them can remain supine and just passive recipients in what God is doing, but in order to enable them to function normally and *do* things. The cripple, the blind man, the lepers, the deaf and dumb man, the mentally ill, those possessed with demons, are freed from the bondage of their afflictions, so that they can go about their business and live normal, active lives. That's so often true when God intervenes in our lives in amazing ways.

That has certainly been my experience. A very moving incident occurred when I was under strict instructions to lie horizontal in a hospital bed. A colleague in our Team Ministry brought his family, and I was asked to bless a small crucifix that his son had been given as a Confirmation present, and to sign the books being given to the candidates. I couldn't even sit up to do either task – I had to bless the crucifix and sign the books lying on my side – but it was a wonderful moment. Then there was the time when another patient who was more mobile than I was, came to sit at my bedside to talk over his own faith questionings. Of course, he knew that I was a priest. The whole ward did: the constant stream of visitors with clerical collars, several of them attached to purple shirts, made that quite obvious! Again, there was the Sunday when two men in adjoining beds to mine decided to join me when I was wheeled to the hospital chapel for the service there (the previous week I had been the only one in the ward to go). God was making it possible for me to *do* things for him in small ways. Without doubt the greatest of all joys was when I hobbled on two sticks into one of the churches where I had been incumbent for more than seventeen years, when I returned to preaching, when I again celebrated Mass, baptized a baby, officiated at weddings and funerals, and was enabled to relieve my dear wife of just a small amount of the heavy burdens she had been carrying for me for months. It was all about being enabled to do things.

The other thing about the Gospel miracles of course is that God acts through and in co-operation with human action: the action of people who bring their friends in need to him on stretchers, and persist in great determination despite all the obstacles; the action of disciples and others asked to do things. God uses what is to hand – the pots of water, the loaves and fishes put at his disposal, and so on. Again, that's always true of his action. It has certainly been my own experience, in the facing of my cancer problems. The combination of the skills and energy of doctors, nurses, therapists and so on with prayer, faith and determination, and the certainty that God's hand is very firmly on the tiller, is what so often brings amazing results. Often it's very hard work, requiring a great deal of perseverance. The invoking of God in a situation isn't to be a passive, supine thing, just leaving it to him and sitting back. There's the classic anecdote of the man greatly given to prayer, who had just missed the bus, and was convinced, if he prayed hard enough, another one would come along quickly. He was so busy concentrating on his prayer, shutting out all the sights and sounds around him, that he didn't notice three buses come and go half empty!

There's another story about the man who was convinced that whatever difficulties he got into, the Lord would save him. One day, he found himself in great difficulty in a lake and likely to drown, and began crying out, 'Lord, help me!' Along came a man in a rowing boat and offered to take him in. He refused, saying 'No, it's alright – the Lord will save me'. Another man came along in a motor launch and offered to help. 'No, it's alright', he said, 'The Lord will save me'. A third man came along in a helicopter and offered to haul him up. 'No', he replied, 'The Lord will save me'. So he drowned; and in heaven he was pretty miffed with God: 'Why didn't you come and save me?' And God replied: 'I sent a man in a rowing boat and another in a launch and another in a helicopter, but you wouldn't take any notice'! So often God uses human beings and human resources to achieve his purposes. It's important to realise that, when we expect him to put everything right with a stroke.

There is one other strand we will see running through the Gospel miracles. Very often they are seen by the evangelists as demonstrating the **glory of God**. In St John's Gospel in particular, the miracles are regarded as illustrations of the statement in the prologue at the outset of the book, 'The Word was made flesh . . . and we beheld his glory' (John 1, v. 14). Having set that marker, the evangelist sets out to demonstrate how the glory of Christ was evident in teaching and action; and the miracles play an important part in doing that. After the turning of the water into wine at Cana, which is the first of the miracles he records, St John comments, 'Jesus performed at Cana in Galilee the first of the signs which revealed his glory'. Then in the discussion leading up to the healing of the blind man in John 9, the Lord says, 'This man was born blind so that God might be glorified in healing him'. That is the tone of the whole Gospel. That element of the demonstration of the glory of God is there throughout all the miracles in the Gospels.

That's really at the heart of things. So often when God is brought into a situation, his love and power are demonstrated in transforming things. It may be in altering the course of events, or it may be in the provision of amazing grace to take us through it. That is why I have chosen to call this little book *Signs Of His Glory*.

As we look in detail at a number of miracles of quite different kinds which are recorded in the Gospels, we will see how those six strands are always there, and how they say a lot to us about our situations today.

II

THE LORD OF WHOLENESS
Miracles of Healing

*'All who had friends ill with diseases
of one kind or another brought them to
him; and he laid his hands on them
one by one, and healed them'*
(Luke 4, v. 49)

In this chapter, we will be looking at miracles in the Gospels involving healing. There are so many such incidents that it can be difficult to know where to begin. Acts of healing not only constitute the overwhelming majority of miracles recorded in the Gospels but their numbers are vast and varied. Incidents like the Healing of the paralysed man (Mark 2, Matthew 9 and Luke 5), the Deliverance of the man possessed with evil spirits, which go into the herd of pigs (Mark 5, Matthew 8 and Luke 8), the Healing of the woman with haemorrhage (Mark 5, Matthew 9 and Luke 8), of the Syro-Phoenician woman's daughter (Mark 7 and Matthew 15) and of the Deaf and dumb man (Mark 7 and Matthew 15) are just a few of the widely varied circumstances in which the miracles occur. We could move about over a great range of miracles, picking out bits from here and there, illustrating different aspects. Instead, however, I am going to look at just three miracles, and see how those six strands are to be found in one way or another in all of them: the need, the humility, the involvement of Christ, the faith, the action, and the demonstration of the glory of God.

The three miracles we will be looking at are the healing of the Blind Man (John 9), the healing of the Centurion's Servant (Matthew 8 and Luke 7) and the healing of the Ten Lepers (Luke 17).

St John devotes a whole chapter of forty verses to the account of the healing of the Blind Man, and the discussion surrounding it. We see the deep moral questionings of the disciples about why the man was born blind and whose fault it was (a question of great concern in a society which was used to identifying illness with uncleanness, and regarding it as a punishment for someone's sin) (John 9, vv. 1–3). We see too, the gossiping among the crowds about the extraordinary events and their significance (vv. 8–12) and the angry interrogation of the man and his family by the Pharisees following the healing, which was part of their hate campaign against Jesus and their refusal to accept him for who he was (vv. 13–34). To understand it all fully, it is helpful to read the whole chapter; but I will quote here from just the first seven verses . . .

> As he went on his way, Jesus saw a man who had been blind from birth. His disciples asked him, 'Rabbi, why was this man born blind? Who sinned, this man or his parents?' 'It is not that he or his parents sinned', Jesus answered, 'He was born blind so that God's power might be displayed in healing him' . . . With these words he spat on the ground and made paste with the spittle; he spread it on the man's eyes, and said to him, 'Go and wash in the pool of Siloam' (The name means 'Sent'.) The man went off and washed, and came back able to see. (John 9, vv. 1–3 and 6–7)

Signs of His Glory

Notice those six strands mentioned here. In this incident, it is Jesus who takes the initiative. The evangelist simply says, 'As he went on his way, Jesus saw a man who had been blind from birth'. The man is just there, quite helpless; he doesn't appear to ask for any change in his lot. The instinct was to think that it was someone's fault – either his or his parents' – that he was blind. That's a natural human instinct – 'What have I done, what has she done, to deserve this?' people will say. The people around just accepted that it was 'one of those things' – it was a fact of life. Folk might pity him and offer him help. The disciples queried *why* it should be so – just as we might about some situation we consider unfair or inexplicable. It seems that there is nothing that can be done about it, nothing that can change things. There is need, weakness, dependency there. Later on in this incident, when Jesus has covered the man's eyes with clay, and tells him to go and wash in the pool of Siloam at the other side of Jerusalem, he would have to be guided there by those prepared to help him. St John says specifically that he 'came back able to see'. The blind man is still helpless and dependent up to that point.

Being led would be a pretty undignified procedure. In fact, the whole situation, the whole process was. St John tells us (v. 8) that he was a beggar who was well known as such. Blind beggars in the street would be a fairly common sight: to their disability and their dependence on sighted people to guide them about would be added the dependence on the charity of passers by for their livelihood. The other three Gospels also record the healing of a blind beggar (in St Mark he is called Bartimaeus) whom Jesus heals instantly. Here, the Lord spits on the ground to make a kind of ointment with the spittle, and smears it on the man's eyes. He tells him to walk, guided no doubt by others, through the crowded city, to wash in the pool of Siloam ... unable to see the looks of the bystanders; only able to imagine them, and to hear their comments . . . 'Look – there's that blind beggar. I wonder what he's up to now, with mud smeared all over his eyes'. There's certainly humility; there can be nothing else.

Like all these incidents of course, it's only when Jesus Christ is brought into things that anything happens. The disciples don't seem to be expecting anything to happen particularly. They are simply remarking on the dilemma, posing the kind of deep questions that people often ask – whose fault it is; why it should happen that this man is in this plight at all. When, however, Our Lord comes on the scene, everything alters. Totally unexpectedly, he takes the initiative, doing something about it. You can imagine some of them saying as he makes the mud and smears it on the blind man's eyes, 'What good does he think *that's* going to do?' But the unexpected happens, and the man receives his sight – because Jesus Christ has been brought into the situation.

Then there's the faith. As is often the case in these incidents, faith goes hand in hand with action. The man is told to go and wash in the pool of Siloam. It sounds so ridiculous – such a stupid thing to do; washing in a pool was such an ordinary and everyday activity. It was an action that must have taken a great deal of faith to think it was worth bothering to do, to make the effort, with his handicap, to get there. So far no change had come over the man's condition; the only change was that his eyes were now covered with a messy clay. You can picture it all: the blind man going, stumbling and fumbling through the streets, guided by others, all the way to the pool. Then the washing in the pool, and he can see! You can imagine how different the return journey is – the man full of jubilation and excitement. Perhaps he returned skipping with joy and shouting out to anyone who was interested, 'I can SEE! I can SEE!' And the effect on his life would be one of action: now he was able to do so much for himself for which up to now he had had to depend on others. The healing enabled him to *do* things.

You can imagine too the effect on the witnesses. The evangelist tells us something of the gossiping that went on ('Isn't this the man that used to sit and beg? Perhaps it's just someone who looks like him. No – it *is* him. How were your eyes opened?') The Pharisees clearly realised what the effect was. That was why they set to work trying to belittle it all, trying to explain it all away, why they were so angry with the healed man and with his parents and why they put them through that hard-hitting interrogation (vv. 13–34). This was very much a sign of the glory of Christ.

The healing of the Centurion's Servant appears in Matthew 8 and Luke 7. I am quoting St Matthew's version; St Luke's version is in Luke 7, vv. 1 to 10 . . .

> As Jesus entered Capernaum, a centurion came up to ask his help. 'Sir', he said, my servant is lying at home paralysed and racked with pain'. Jesus said, 'I will come and cure him'. But the centurion replied, 'Sir, I am not worthy to have you under my roof. You need only say the word and my servant will be cured. I know, for I am myself under orders, with soldiers under me. I say to one, "Go", and he goes; to another, "Come", and he comes; to my servant, "Do this", and he does it'. Jesus heard him with astonishment, and said, 'Truly I tell you, nowhere in Israel have I found such faith'. Then Jesus said to the centurion, 'Go home; and, as you have believed, so let it be'. At that very moment, the boy recovered. (Matthew 8, vv. 5–10 and 13)

Again, there are the six strands. To start with, there is the need, the helplessness: the recognition that there is nothing the centurion can do about it, despite the resources at his command. It is useless his giving any commands, any orders about this situation, for all that he is used to giving orders to soldiers. It is a simple, bald statement, 'My servant is lying at home, paralysed and racked with pain'. It is not clear from either this account or the version in Luke 7 what the cause of the paralysis is, or how extensive it is. The only things that are clear are that it is causing great pain and distress, and that there appears to be nothing that can be done about it. The centurion, though a tough soldier, and used to the afflictions of war, shows great compassion for his servant; and he feels totally helpless to do anything about his condition.

Then there is the humility involved. A centurion was not a particularly high ranking officer in the Roman army – he would have command of between fifty and a hundred men; but he was, as he says, a man used to both carrying out orders and giving orders and a representative in a small way of the power and authority of the Roman Empire. But this counts for nothing. In St Luke's version of this incident, the centurion does not, as a Gentile, presume to approach the Lord himself but sends some Jewish friends. They plead on his behalf, citing his reputation as a friend of Israel, 'Who has built us a synagogue'. (This in itself suggests that he was a man of some substance). In St Matthew's account, he comes himself. No doubt both approaches take place, so dire is the situation and so worried is he. But this centurion comes to Jesus, not demanding, in the manner that he would give orders to his soldiers, or pointing to his religious good works, but simply telling Jesus what the problem is; in humility laying it all out before him. Then when the Lord offers to go and heal the servant, he replies with those classic words, which have subsequently found their way into liturgical use as an acclamation before Holy Communion 'Lord I am not worthy that you should come under my roof'.

The healing of the centurion's servant is different in some

ways from many other healing miracles in that it is one of the few instances where the Lord does not actually come into contact with the sick man: it is a healing as it were 'by remote control', rather like the healing of the Syro-Phoenician woman's daughter in Mark 7 and Matthew 15, or the nobleman's son in John 4, other examples of people coming to Jesus asking for healing for someone else. In some ways, that is one factor that makes the incident all the more amazing. Nevertheless it is the fact that Jesus Christ is brought into the situation that alters it so dramatically. The evangelist is careful to point out that 'At that very moment, the boy recovered'.

The faith involved in this incident is enormous. The Lord himself remarks on it as he often does on these occasions. 'Truly', he says, 'nowhere in Israel have I found such faith'. The nature of the centurion's faith is underlined by the fact that he expresses it without prompting. In fact the Lord is ready to go to the servant's bedside to effect the cure and offers to do so; it is the centurion who says there is no need so long as Jesus gives the word. Again, that ties up with the action: in this case making the journey back to the sick boy's bedside (at his own suggestion!) with the conviction that all will be well. Presumably, having been cured, the servant resumes his role in the centurion's service. That is the whole point of what has happened – to enable him to be active again.

The account of this incident in both Matthew and Luke ends here. There is no further reference to the effect it had on the centurion's household or on the witnesses of what had happened. We can only speculate on that; but the likelihood is that it made a deep impression on them all, that this too was an incident that glorified God.

Lepers, and the healing of lepers appear several times in

the Gospels. One incident that must have made a great impact on the witnesses is the Healing of the Ten Lepers in Luke 17.

> As he was entering a village he was met by ten men with leprosy. They stood some way off and called out to him 'Jesus, Master, take pity on us'. When he saw them, he said, 'Go and show yourselves to the priests'; and while they were on their way they were made clean. One of them, finding himself cured, turned back with shouts of praise to God. He threw himself down at Jesus's feet and thanked him. And he was a Samaritan. At this Jesus said, 'Were there not ten made clean? The other nine where are they? Was no-one found returning to give praise to God except this foreigner?' And he said to the man, 'Stand up and go on your way; your faith has cured you. (Luke 17 vv. 12–19)

Again, we can see those six strands. This was certainly a situation of helplessness. Leprosy was a dreaded disease that was painful and ugly and considered to be a certain death warrant; lepers were regarded, more than those suffering from any other affliction, as being 'unclean'. The ten men standing apart and shouting out as the Lord and his followers walked by would be a pathetic sight. It would not be an unusual thing to see lepers in the street begging for scraps to be thrown to them like dogs. They could not live a normal life and earn their living in a normal way, because they were excluded from society. And there was no escape for them – no one would expect for a moment that they could be cured. It was just one of those things; a fact of life that had to be accepted.

Inevitably, their plight went hand in hand with an enforced humility because society shunned them out of fear. Until recent times, this was always the case. Often in the Middle Ages, lepers were expected to wear a bell so as to warn people of their approach and give them a chance to keep well clear.

Signs of His Glory

When medical missionaries got involved with treating and caring for lepers, it was considered both revolutionary and courageous. So the lepers in this incident are 'standing some way off', because society compelled them to do so. But, there is more to the humility of these men than that. Our natural instinct would be to complain, to cry out, 'Why me?' to demand to be released from the unfairness of it. These lepers don't say that: they stand at a distance, simply crying out, 'Jesus, Master, take pity on us!' They don't even appear to ask for a cure; they simply ask for his pity, his mercy. Maybe they aren't presuming to ask for release from their imprisonment to the leprosy, but simply asking for a coin or a scrap of food, as they are used to asking from any passer by, so accustomed have they become to begging. The humility and humiliation of these men is total.

Again, it is the involvement of Jesus Christ that changes everything and achieves what no one would have imagined possible, or even thought of seeking. As the lepers shout from the distance for some kind of help in their plight, Jesus takes the initiative, takes charge of things and the unthinkable happens. The dreaded, insurmountable affliction of leprosy is overcome, and all ten men are healed.

And again, the faith and action involved in this incident are quite amazing. The ten men are told to 'go and show yourselves to the priests'. The purpose of that in a society where the priests would also act in a sense as something akin to medical officers of health, would be to be given a 'clean bill of health'. This would enable them to be accepted back into society again to live normal lives and to earn their living like anyone else. What they were being asked to do is really quite extraordinary. When they set off to the priests following the Lord's instructions, no change in their condition appears to have taken place: the evangelist tells us quite specifically,

Signs of His Glory

'While they were on their way, they were made clean'. The ten lepers were asked to do a quite illogical, crazy thing. Logic would seem to put into their minds the question, 'What's the point? Surely the priests will turn us away and accuse us of wasting their time, or trying to deceive them!' It would take a great deal of faith and trust simply to do what Jesus asked them to do.

Then there was the one man who turned back to say 'Thank you'. Only one of them, you notice. In fact, the Lord himself remarks on such a low percent rating of gratitude, and the fact that the one man who did return was a Samaritan, who to pious Jews of the time was a member of a despised race: 'The other nine, where are they? Was no one found returning to give praise to God except this foreigner?' But one man does return; so that this miracle is also often used as a parable of gratitude and thankfulness. We can imagine the scene as St Luke describes it vividly, telling us that the man returned 'with shouts of praise to God', and threw himself down at the Lord's feet thanking him. Again, the glory of God is shown.

In this chapter, we have looked at just three out of a whole range of healing miracles in the Gospels. It would be possible of course to look at many more in the same way; but I hope the appetite might have been whetted to discover more of what is to be found in these accounts. So what relevance can they have for us? It all comes down to where I began, with that throw away remark, 'I won't say it's a miracle ...'. The word miracle is used so lightly at times: it slips easily off the tongue in everyday conversation to describe something that takes us by surprise or overwhelms us; it even gets slipped into television advertisements to describe the unbelievable properties of some product or other! At the same time, the idea of serious belief in the miraculous is dismissed out of hand, as sitting uneasily beside a world of technology and secularism. But there are many situations in life in which God acts powerfully, where the effect of faithful prayer is strongly evident and in which those six strands we have been discovering in the Gospel miracles are to be found.

I have already written something about my own personal experiences of the powerful effect of prayer and of the action of God in my own situation of illness, and of my huge sense of gratitude for my experience of the last two and a half years or so. Twelve months after my discharge from hospital, I made a personal pilgrimage of thanksgiving to the Shrine of Our Lady of Walsingham; and it was one of the most meaningful of the many visits to that wonderful place of pilgrimage since I discovered it as a student over forty years ago. I had so much for which to thank God, as I walked down to the Holy Well for sprinkling and lit candles in the Holy House.

Of course, it is not always like that: sometimes we feel that God disappoints us, that what he does isn't what we would want him to do, or what faith leads us to expect. We are bewildered when a good and faithful priest is murdered by someone he is endeavouring to help – when we read the account of a whole congregation slaughtered as they are gathered in their church for Mass during an ethnic civil war, with everyone desperately trying to receive Communion before they fall to the machine guns – when children in a school are mown down by a lunatic gunman – when someone very close to us dies after a long illness through which we have held them in prayer . . . the list is endless. At those moments we are devastated, and we ask the perennial question, 'Why?' And yet God does often act powerfully – either to change the direction of things, or to take us through them.

All the time there are those six strands present: the need and helplessness and our awareness of it, and the humility of recognising our need and dependence in the context of a world and a society in which it is thought that men and women can cope with and be in control of literally everything. There is the faith, sometimes against all the odds (again in a world in which faith is not fashionable, in which it comes under all kinds of cynical pressures) and the confidence to act in that faith, sometimes in ways in which we surprise ourselves and in ways the world considers crazy or pointless. Finally there is the realisation that when Jesus Christ is brought into a situation, things can change dramatically; and the instinct to praise and thank God for the powerful way in which he so often acts.

III
THE LORD OF THE PRACTICAL
Miracles of Food and Drink

'Do whatever he tells you'
(John 2, v. 5)

In this chapter, we will be looking at some miracles of quite a different kind which appear in the Gospels. Unlike the healing miracles they are not responses to matters of life and death, or the desperate need of those in sickness and distress. They occur in situations mainly of frustration, embarrassment and inconvenience (in one instance, touching on men's livelihood). They are all incidents involving Food and Drink. I am going to look closely at three such miracles: the Turning of Water into Wine at the wedding at Cana in Galilee (John 2); the Feeding of the Multitude which appears in all four Gospels; and the Miraculous Draught of Fish (Luke 5). In each incident we will be looking for those six strands: the need, the humility, the effect of the involvement of Christ, the faith needed, the action expected of people and the glory of God that is displayed. Then we will see how these incidents say things to us about life as we know it.

The incident at the Wedding at Cana in Galilee only appears

Signs of His Glory

in St John's Gospel; and the evangelist refers to it as 'the first of the signs that revealed the glory of Christ'.

> Two days later there was a wedding at Cana in Galilee. The mother of Jesus was there and Jesus and his disciples were also among the guests. The wine gave out, so Jesus's mother said to him 'They have no wine left'. He answered, 'That is no concern of mine. My hour has not yet come.' His mother said to the servants 'Do whatever he tells you.' There were six stone water-jars standing near of the kind used for Jewish rites of purification; each held from twenty to thirty gallons. Jesus said to the servants, 'Fill the jars with water,' and they filled them to the brim. 'Now draw some off', he ordered, 'and take it to the master of the feast'; and they did so. The master tasted the water, now turned into wine, not knowing its source, though the servants who drew the water knew. He hailed the bridegroom and said 'Everyone else serves the best wine first and the poorer when the guests have drunk freely; but you have kept the best wine till now'. So Jesus performed at Cana in Galilee the first of the signs which revealed his glory and led his disciples to believe in him. (John 2, vv. 1–11)

This may seem in some ways a more frivolous incident than those we looked at in the previous chapter. The situation is one of embarrassment rather than real need. Those organising the wedding reception have run out of wine – perhaps because of bad planning, or because more people have turned up than expected (maybe with some gatecrashers), perhaps because the guests have drunk more freely than expected. For whatever reason, there is acute embarrassment, and the possibility that the newly-weds' special day will be spoilt. So there is a kind of need; a need because in some way or other mistakes have been made or there have been unexpected developments. Notice that in this instance, as far as we know, people don't actually ask for anything to be done about it. The approach to Our Lord doesn't come from the organisers or the waiters or the bridegroom or the relatives: it is Mary his mother who brings it to his attention. She is the intercessor for others; which is symbolical of her role in Christian tradition. To start with, Our Lord seems to brush her aside – 'That's no concern of mine'. You wonder whether the servants referred to overheard that conversation. If so, they might well have thought to themselves that there was no use pursuing *that* line. Mary too, for that matter – her concern seeming to be totally brushed aside. But she simply says to them 'Do whatever he tells you'. The need and the humility go hand in hand.

Then we notice that as with all these miracles it is the involvement of *Jesus* that transforms everything. It is interesting that the Lord is seen at this wedding feast at Cana. Why he and his mother and the disciples were among the guests, we are not told. Maybe it was some family connection or friendship. The newly-weds are not identified; so we have no idea what the connection might have been. The important thing here is that the Lord is shown entering into the joy of the occasion, the happiness of the newly-weds and the general jollification – and making sure, by his action in the crisis, that a damper isn't put on the happy day. It reminds us that he is concerned about ordinary, practical things, and also about the important moments in people's lives, that he approves of celebrations and parties. Nevertheless, the most important thing, as with all these incidents is, that bringing Jesus into situations makes all the difference.

As we have already seen, faith and action are crucial in all these episodes; and that is certainly so at Cana. Here again, the two go hand in hand. The waiters are asked to do something quite ridiculous. Mary says to them, 'Do whatever he tells you', and what Jesus said must have flabbergasted them: 'Fill the water pots with water, and take that to the table for them to drink'. To human intelligence it sounds a quite stupid idea, indeed an outrageous suggestion. Until Jesus was brought into the equation no one would have dreamt of taking such a bizarre step. We can imagine what might have gone through their minds . . . 'Surely they cannot be so drunk that they won't realise that a fast one is being pulled on them; surely they can still tell the difference between water and wine! We'll be laughing stocks; or worse still, ticked off or even sacked!' But amazingly for all their misgivings the waiters still do what Jesus tells them. That quite outrageous, illogical action would take a great deal of trust, and faith that it was worth doing what he said.

The effect of their action is quite amazing. 'The master of the feast, tasting the water now turned into wine . . .' writes St John. The evangelist refers to the transformation almost casually. He alludes to it in passing almost as an after thought in parenthesis; and he goes on to record that the master of the feast remarks, 'You have kept the best wine until now'. In our terminology, it is not just cheap plonk, the most inexpensive off the supermarket shelf, brought on after people's tastebuds have been blunted, but equivalent to the best claret or champagne! And the quantity is *vast*: six stone water jars, each containing between twenty and thirty gallons. Altogether that is about 150 gallons or more than a thousand bottles. That's an awful lot of wine. You wonder how many there were at that party to be able to consume that much wine! Of course that isn't the point: the measurements are not recorded so that we can work out how much water or wine was involved. What this incident is telling us is that what is produced when Jesus Christ is brought into the picture and his instructions are carried out, is both the best that can possibly be had, and limitless in quantity. In this amazing way the glory of Christ is displayed.

The Feeding of the Five Thousand appears in various forms in all four Gospels (Mark 6 vv. 35–44, Matthew 14 vv. 15–21, Luke 9 vv. 12–17, and John 6, vv. 1–14). St Matthew also has the Feeding of the Four Thousand (Chapter 15). The version in John 6 gives us the most personal detail ...

> Some time later, Jesus withdrew to the farther shore of the sea of Galilee (or Tiberias), and a large crowd of people followed him because they had seen the signs he performed in healing the sick. Jesus went up the hillside and sat down with his disciples. It was near the time of Passover, the great Jewish festival. Looking up and seeing a large crowd coming towards him, Jesus said to Philip, 'Where are we to buy bread to feed these people?' He said this to test him: Jesus himself knew what he meant to do. Philip replied, 'We would need two hundred denarii to buy enough bread for each of them to have a little'. One of his disciples, Andrew, the brother of Simon Peter, said to him, 'There is a boy here who has five barley loaves and two fish; but what is that among so many?' Jesus said, 'Make the people sit down'. There was plenty of grass there, so the men sat down, about five thousand of them. Then Jesus took the loaves, gave thanks, and distributed them to the people as they sat there. He did the same with the fish, and they had as much as they wanted. When everyone had had enough, he said to his disciples, 'Gather up the pieces left over, so that nothing is wasted'. They gathered them up, and filled twelve baskets with the pieces of the five barley loaves that were left uneaten. When the people saw the sign Jesus had performed, the word went round, 'Surely this must be the Prophet who was to come into the world'. (John 6, vv. 1–14)

Again, we can see those six strands. To start with the situation presents the disciples with a dilemma. People have been following Jesus around and listening to him for a long time, and they are getting hungry. St Mark says of this incident, 'It was already getting late'. St Matthew and St Luke say that it was evening, and St John refers to it being 'near the time of Passover', when all trading would cease as people got down to the serious business of keeping the festival. Three of the evangelists refer to it being a remote or desert place. So there are all kinds of practical obstacles. It is the Lord who takes the initiative. In fact Matthew, Mark and Luke all say that the disciples pressed him to send the people away to get their own food. But Jesus takes the initiative in putting that question to Philip, 'Where are we to buy bread to feed these people?' Philip seems to indicate it is a quite ridiculous idea even thinking about it, remarking on how much money it would take to buy enough food 'for each of them to take a little'. The money is irrelevant: what is being pointed out is what a huge catering operation it would be. In human terms, the prospect of feeding that vast multitude seems totally impractical. Then Andrew mentions the loaves and fishes. The way he mentions them is almost apologetic, as much as to say, 'It's a very long shot, and quite ridiculous really, but there's nothing else' – 'What is that among so many?' It is a recognition that in human terms, the prospect of doing anything about the situation is hopeless; there is nothing that *can* be done. It is beyond them; they can only give up, and leave people to their own resources to go and find food where they can.

Again it is the involvement of Christ that makes that impossible, ridiculous idea not only possible but amazingly successful. While they are reflecting on the impossibility of the situation, on the vast nature of the problem and the ridiculously limited resources available, Jesus just acts quite simply, blessing the loaves and fishes for distribution. Again, you notice they are asked to do something. Matthew Mark and Luke all tell us that the Lord gave the blessed food to the disciples, for them to distribute to the crowds. It's something that their logic would clearly suggest to them was ridiculous and likely to be totally ineffective. There's that same faith in action again.

It is all part too, of the fact that Jesus uses what is to hand, what is put at his disposal. As with the water at Cana, so with the loaves and fishes that Andrew hadn't really been seriously suggesting because of their inadequacy. In each case that was all there was available. In St John's account, we have that interesting personal touch of the boy who surrenders his picnic basket. In the other accounts, the loaves and fishes are only referred to as all they have available. Here we are told that they come from a boy who has brought them with him and surrenders them for the Lord to use. Maybe the boy offered them himself; maybe Andrew looking round spotted the boy and asked for the food. Whichever way it happened, the contents of the picnic basket were put at the Lord's disposal and he used them to feed the crowd.

And again, the outcome is quite amazing. People have tried to explain it all away. It has been suggested for instance that it was really like one of those 'shared suppers' (a fellowship meal in which everyone brings some food and it is all shared out). The crowd all had their 'sandwiches', and they were brought out at the appropriate moment and passed round. The boy with the picnic basket was only one of many who had come so prepared; and the only miracle was in persuading people to share. This runs quite contrary to the general tenor of the account and the references that are made to this incident elsewhere in the Gospels. The extraordinary nature of it all is what comes through, starting with the statement 'Jesus himself knew what he meant to do'. Not only do five thousand people have a satisfactory meal off five small loaves (in our terms not much more than tea cakes) and two fish but they afterwards fill twelve baskets with the scraps left over. In other words there appears to be much more left over than there was to start with! Again, it demonstrates the glory of Christ.

The account of the Miraculous Draught of Fish is to be found in Luke 5 . . .

> When he had finished speaking, he said to Simon 'Put out into deep water and let down your nets for a catch'. Simon answered 'Master we were hard at work all night and caught nothing; but if you say so we will let down the nets'. They did so, and made such a huge catch of fish that their nets began to split. So they signalled to their partners in the other boat to come and help them. They came and loaded both boats to the point of sinking. When Simon saw what had happened he fell at Jesus's knees, and said, 'Go, Lord. Leave me, sinner that I am!' For he and all his companions were amazed at the catch they had made; so too were his partners James and John, Zebedee's sons. 'Do not be afraid' said Jesus to Simon; 'From now on you will be catching people'. As soon as they had brought the boats to land, they left everything and followed him. (Luke 5, vv. 4–11)

You can see those six strands in this one too. To start with, there is that sense of failure, of disappointment, among the fishermen. Jesus has come along at a particularly sensitive moment, and asked to be allowed to use one of their boats as a kind of makeshift pulpit from which to speak to the crowds (Luke 5, v. 3). You can imagine the fishermen listening as they see to the washing and mending of their nets after a frustratingly unsuccessful night in which they haven't caught a single fish. To them that would be vital since they made their living from catching fish. They listen to Jesus's teaching about the Kingdom of Heaven and the good news of the

Signs of His Glory

Gospel against the background of their own very practical problems and frustrations, perhaps wondering what it has got to do with them, and how it can possibly affect them. Then Jesus asks them to put out to sea, and let down their nets again for a catch. No doubt their professional instinct is to ask what does *he* know about it? They are the experts; they know better. They have already used all the tricks of the trade, and there are no fish to be had. He must be 'talking through his hat', as we say. Anyway, whatever their thoughts are, Peter simply says 'Master, we were hard at work all night and caught nothing; nevertheless if *you* say so I will let down the nets'. There has to be a real humility in the readiness of the expert fishermen who know those waters so well, to do what Jesus says.

Again, the factor that totally changes things is Jesus Christ. Up until the moment when *he* comes on the scene it's just one of those days when there's no catch. They have to accept the inevitable; they are used to doing that. Then the Lord takes the initiative. Perhaps, while he is teaching the crowds, he can hear the fishermen talking among themselves, complaining about what an unproductive night it has been. At any rate he tells them to cast the nets again; and when they do, there is such a huge haul of fish that the nets begin to split, and they need help to get it all ashore. Things are turned totally around because Jesus Christ is involved. Again, some people will try to explain it away suggesting that it was all coincidence, that there happened to be a great movement of fish at that moment. There may well have been; but from their reaction the fishermen clearly thought there was more to it than that – and they were the experts, experienced in fishing those waters and who knew all about the fish and where to find them.

Of course there is faith involved in the disciples' readiness to act. The way the Lord deals with the situation isn't just to make a gesture of blessing and invocation over the sea and the nets, but to ask them to do something in faith. It is something that their logic and professional expertise might tell them is pointless and likely to be fruitless. As always with these Gospel miracles it isn't their faith and trust and readiness to act that actually creates the miracle – it is God's action that does that – but it is their faith and trust and readiness to act that makes it possible for them to avail themselves of what he does. If they had refused to do what he asked – if they had responded, 'You must be joking, man; we can't be bothered doing something so pointless', nothing further would have happened.

The other noticeable thing of course is the effect the miracle has on them. Peter, a fisherman who knows all about the sea and its resources, falls down in front of Jesus, saying, 'Go, Lord; leave me, sinner that I am.' He is so aware of the presence and glory of God that he has just witnessed that he cannot cope with it, and wants to put it all away from him. In fear, he just asks Jesus to go away. The Lord reassures him, telling him not to be afraid and that he will be a fisher of men; and then all four fishermen forsake their nets and follow Jesus from that moment. They become the nucleus of the apostolic ministry and of the mission of the Christian Church.

So what do these incidents say to us about how God acts? The first thing to realise is that God cares about ordinary, mundane, everyday situations. In fact he is in the middle of them with us all the time. That is at the heart of the Christian belief about the Person of Christ, Jesus who is God Incarnate. He is not a faraway God but a God who acts and makes himself known in the everyday: a God for instance who acts powerfully through Sacraments. So there is nothing that is outside his concern. There are so many issues and problems and needs that weigh heavily on our hearts. In the face of them we feel totally helpless, as we watch the TV news or read our newspapers, with the constant train of disasters, outrages and intractable dilemmas, or as we cope with problems and crises affecting ourselves or those who are close and important to us. Nevertheless *all* of those concerns are his concerns as well as ours.

So we bring it all to him. Just as at Cana Jesus's Mother brought the problem of the wedding party so we will bring problems of others, large or small, to him, interceding for a marriage in difficulties, a crucial examination, a redundancy, the collapse of a business, a drug problem, a career disappointment . . . and many other things. Being an intercessor for someone is one of the most powerful, valuable and effective things we can do. I know that from personal experience; I have been strongly aware of the many people who have prayed for me and of the effectiveness of that prayer. Just as Philip and Andrew discussed with Jesus the hugeness and insurmountability of the problem facing them, and the total inadequacy of the resources available, or Peter and the others bemoaned the night they had spent unproductively fishing the sea, so the most difficult and intractable problems ought most of all to be brought to the Lord in prayer.

We know how weak and helpless we so often are – and so is humanity for that matter – and how dependent we are on God's grace and power. We also know that he uses what is to hand and what is put at his disposal, like the pots of water at Cana, or the loaves and fishes or the fishermen's boats and nets. God does that too in the Sacraments. In the Eucharist he takes what is put at his disposal – the bread and wine that are the products of the earth and of human work – and uses them to give us his own life. That in itself is miraculous. And he often acts through us. It's important to remember that, when we bemoan some situation and expect God to do something about it, or complain that he allows dreadful things to happen, or when the phrase 'an act of God' is trotted out because there is no one else to blame for some disaster. At those moments it may be that God is inspiring *us* to do something about it. Then sometimes he expects us to take steps of faith that don't seem at all logical or likely to be productive, and we are tempted to think we know better.

At the end of the day many things redound to God's glory. There are of course plenty of things we come across which seem to deny his Lordship of all creation or his purposes of love: times and situations where ugliness and distress and cruelty and wickedness seem triumphant and we are bewildered by it all. Nevertheless there are also many times when quite the opposite is the case; when God's love and concern and his hand on the tiller become overwhelmingly evident. Those times are real Signs Of His Glory. This is especially evident when he takes and uses the skills, energies and commitment of faithful men and women who have put themselves at his disposal.

IV

THE LORD OF CREATION
Miracles of the Natural Elements

'Take heart! It is I; be not afraid'
(Matthew 14, v. 27)

So far, we have looked at miracles of healing, and those involving food and drink. In this chapter, we will be looking at some miracles involving the Natural Elements: the Calming of the Storm, which appears in three Gospels (Matthew, Mark and Luke); the Walking on the Water, which appears in Mark and Matthew; and the Transfiguration, which appears in Matthew, Mark and Luke.

Of course, these days we tend to regard nature in a more cavalier fashion than former generations did: we tend to think that it is ours to control, and the developments of technology mean that more things are within our control all the time. Still, there are times when the hugeness, powerfulness and untamed nature of it all, and our minuteness beside it, become very evident. To stand on the top of somewhere like the Longmynd in Shropshire, buffeted by gusting winds with rolling hills stretching for miles in all directions, or look out across the extent of some beautiful tarn in the Lake District is a breathtaking and humbling experience that puts so much in perspective. To be caught in the middle of a massive thunderstorm can have the same effect, and be quite terrifying, as it puts us firmly in our place and cuts us down to size.

The Gospel incidents we will be looking at are ones where the powerful presence of Christ cuts right through such things in amazing ways. These incidents run quite contrary to the normal way things would be. They seem totally unnatural – or supernatural! Those who witness them would never have dreamt of things happening the way they do; they run totally contrary to their experience of things. We will notice, too, that in all of the accounts there is an element of fear – partly leading up to the incident, but certainly as a result of experiencing it. In addition, in all three incidents we will find those six strands we have found in the other miracles: the weakness, fragility and need leading up to the incident; the humility of those who are in that situation; the centrality of Christ to it all, the way his involvement in the situation transforms it dramatically; the faith required for people to benefit from what he does, the action (sometimes quite ridiculous) required of them; and the effect of the incident. Most of all, we see the demonstration of the glory of Christ, the fact that these incidents are all Signs of his Glory.

We are going to start with the incident of the Calming of the Storm. It is common to three Gospels, appearing in Mark 4, vv. 35–41, Matthew 8, vv. 23-27 and Luke 8, vv. 22–25. St Matthew describes it thus . . .

> Jesus then got into the boat, and his disciples followed. All at once, a great storm arose in the lake, till the waves were breaking right over the boat; but he went on sleeping. So they came and woke him up, saying: 'Save us, Lord; we are sinking!' 'Why are you such cowards?', he said, 'How little faith you

have!' With that he got up and rebuked the wind and the sea, and there was a dead calm. The men were astonished at what had happened, and exclaimed, 'What sort of man is this? Even the wind and the sea obey him'. (Matthew 8, vv. 23–27)

This is one of those very dramatic Gospel incidents, which we can picture vividly. The first thing to notice is the weakness of the men in the boat, tossed about on huge waves, which threaten to smash it to pieces like a little matchbox. If you have ever been at sea, even in a liner, in a real storm, you know that it is no fun. I remember many years ago being in the notorious Bay of Biscay, my first ever such journey, when a real humdinger of a storm blew up. The ship we were in was a pretty large and sturdy floating object; but it was literally rolling from side to side, with huge waves washing over the deck. I have to admit, that like many others on their first trip through the Bay of Biscay, I was sick over the side! A fishing boat of course is a much lighter and more fragile vessel than that – particularly the kind of boat that would be out fishing on the Sea of Galilee. Thus those men in the little fishing boat in the storm feel very weak and fragile. They are terrified. And Jesus is there in the boat; but he is *asleep*! In desperation, they wake him up. The way St Mark puts it in his account, they seem somewhat miffed that he is sleeping through the storm while everyone is scared out of their wits, and they wake him up with some irritation saying, 'We are sinking! Don't you care?' (Mark 4, v. 38). In St Luke's version, they simply burst out as they wake him, 'Master, Master! We are sinking!' Here in St Matthew's account, there is the straightforward plea for help, 'Save us, Lord; we are sinking!'. They know they are in a fix and there is no way they are going to get themselves out of it; and so they turn to the Lord.

What happens next is quite amazing; that's certainly how *they* see it at any rate. You wonder what they expect the Lord to do when they wake him up in desperation pleading, 'Save us!'; because what he does clearly amazes them. With a word, he calms the storm, and what has been a raging sea with huge terrifying waves becomes as quiet as a millpond. In a way, it's like leaving the stormy Bay of Biscay behind you and sailing through the straits of Gibraltar into the calm of the Mediterranean – except that it happens in the same place in a split second at a single word of command! Of course, the cynical would say that there just happened to be a sudden calming of the way the sea was behaving – something not all that unusual with the Sea of Galilee. Yet these are men who are used to the behaviour of that sea, which they fish regularly, and they are obviously really amazed at what has happened. Again, what has made the difference is the bringing of Christ into the situation.

As usual, faith features a great deal in this incident – this time in a quite different way. So often in the context of the Gospel miracles, the Lord remarks on the greatness of the faith displayed; here it is quite the opposite. 'How little faith you have', he says, when they come to him in panic, before he proceeds to calm the storm. Then, unlike so many of the miracles, he doesn't ask them to do anything, except to have faith and not to panic – though that is a lot to ask in that situation! Then, after the calming of the storm, all they are asked to do is to take things on from that point – to continue taking the boat on to their destination, to take it all in their stride.

The final word in all three accounts of this incident is about their amazement, their reflection on the Person who is in their midst doing such astounding things: 'They were astonished, and exclaimed, 'What sort of man is this? Even the wind and the sea obey him'. This is very much a sign of his glory.

Signs of His Glory

Another incident of this kind is the Walking on the Water, which appears in Mark 6, vv. 45–52 and Matthew 14, vv. 22–33. St Matthew's version reads . . .

> As soon as they had finished, he made the disciples embark and cross to the other side ahead of him, while he dismissed the crowd; then he went up the hill by himself to pray. It had grown late, and he was there alone. The boat was already some distance from the shore, battling with a head wind and rough sea. Between three and six in the morning, he came towards them, walking across the lake. When the disciples saw him walking on the lake, they were so shaken that they cried out in terror: 'It is a ghost!' But at once Jesus spoke to them: 'Take heart: it is I; be not afraid.' Peter called to him, 'Lord, if it is you, tell me to come to you over the water'. 'Come', said Jesus. Peter got down out of the boat, and walked over the water towards Jesus. But when he saw the strength of the gale he was afraid; and beginning to sink, he cried, 'Save me, Lord!' Jesus at once reached out and caught hold of him. 'Why did you hesitate?', he said, 'How little faith you have!' Then he climbed into the boat, and the wind dropped. And the men in the boat fell at his feet, exclaiming, 'You must be the Son of God'. (Matthew 14, vv. 22–33)

Another storm at sea kind of situation! It's not as dangerous as the one in the incident of the Calming of the Storm of course; but certainly one that emphasises the weakness and fragility of men in a little boat at the mercy of the elements. In St Mark's account, we are told that they are 'labouring at the oars against a head wind'; St Matthew here tells us that they are 'battling with a head wind and rough sea'. However, the incident here is not about stormy weather conditions; it's about the walking on the water.

It starts with the disciples out there without Jesus. The elements around them seem so daunting and enormous, separating them so definitely from the land, where they have left the Lord alone, praying. The last thing they have experienced is the Feeding of the Multitude. No doubt the wonder of that amazing experience is still lingering in their minds; but now they are on their own. And they are so small and weak; the elements are so huge and insurmountable. Then the Lord comes to them walking on the water, doing something that seems quite impossible: not treading water, as you might do at the seaside, but walking on top of it! To start with, they don't actually grasp that it *is* Jesus. Both accounts tell us that they think it is a ghost. It is between three and six in the morning. Perhaps their imagination is playing tricks on them in the dark: the whole thing seems so impossible, because it's a complete reversal of the natural order of things. As he so often does, Jesus Christ turns things upside down.

Then there's that sudden surge of faith experienced by St Peter: that mad request, 'Lord, if it is you, tell me to come to you over the water'. Amazingly, when Jesus gives the word, Peter steps out of the relative security of the boat onto the water, and walks towards him. Then he looks down at the swirling waves, starts thinking logically again and says to himself, 'What am I doing? This is crazy!'. From that moment, he starts to sink, and the Lord has to lift him up. Reading this passage takes me back to my time in hospital, when I had to learn afresh how to walk, following the treatment for cancer on my spine. Simply to take a few steps and keep my balance was a major achievement that took a great deal of confidence; and the first time I tried to walk without a stick, I collapsed into the doctor's arms. It was largely a matter of confidence. So with Peter, it is when his confidence fails that he sinks, when he thinks the whole thing is totally impractical; and that happens when he takes his eyes off Jesus and looks instead at the practical, the insurmountable difficulty, the thing that seems impossible. Then the Lord says to Peter, 'Why did you hesitate? How little faith you have!' It mirrors the comment at the time of the Calming of the Storm. To start with, Peter *has* faith – faith enough to step out, his eyes fixed on the Lord – and his readiness to take that crazy step of leaving the relative security of the boat and walking on the waves is the vehicle God uses to demonstrate his power. In human, natural terms, it is such a mad, pointless thing to do; and sure enough, when he starts thinking in those terms, he loses his nerve and starts sinking. Then the Lord intervenes, extends a hand and lifts Peter up, and they both step into the boat. Again, Jesus's intervention transforms everything.

The effect of course is quite amazing. As with the Calming of the Storm, there is fear – fear of the elements, fear when they first see the Lord walking on the water and think they have seen a ghost, fear on Peter's part when he thinks he is going to drown and most of all, fear when they realise what an amazing thing has happened. The account ends on that note of the reaction of the disciples, 'You must be the Son of God'. Yet again, here is a miracle that is a sign of his glory.

The Transfiguration, like the Calming of the Storm, appears in three Gospels (Mark 9, vv. 2–10, Matthew 17, vv. 1–9 and Luke 9, vv. 28–36). St Matthew describes it thus:-

> Six days later, Jesus took Peter, James and John the brother of James, and led them up a high mountain by themselves. And in their presence he was transfigured; his face shone like the sun, and his clothes became a brilliant white. And they saw Moses and Elijah appear, talking with him. Then Peter spoke: 'Lord', he said, 'It is good that we are here. Would you like me to make three shelters here, one for you, one for Moses, and one for Elijah?' While he was speaking, a bright cloud suddenly cast its shadow over them, and a voice called from the cloud:

Signs of His Glory

'This is my beloved Son in whom I delight: listen to him'. At the sound of the voice the disciples fell on their faces in terror. Then Jesus came up to them, touched them and said, 'Stand up; do not be afraid.' And when they raised their eyes, there was no one but Jesus to be seen. On their way down the mountain, Jesus commanded them not to tell anyone of the vision until the Son of Man had been raised from the dead. (Matthew 17, vv. 1–9)

This is a quite different kind of incident from the miracles we have been thinking about, and it may seem strange to include it in this chapter because it is spiritual in nature. It is an experience that a small group of the followers of Jesus Christ are given, to help them become more deeply aware of him and who he is. It is a vision. Yet it is a miracle, for all that, because it transcends the normal limitations of human experience; and those six strands highlighted in previous accounts are to be found in this one too.

To start with, the miracle comes against the background of the gathering fear and uncertainty about what the future holds. In St Luke's account of the Transfiguration, the function of Moses and Elijah is to speak of the coming Passion – 'they spoke of his departure, of the coming destiny he was to fulfil in Jerusalem' (Luke 9, v. 31) – and the whole experience of the Transfiguration emphasises the disciples' impotence. The experience is so unexpected, so out of the ordinary, that they don't know what to do; and Peter fumblingly speaks of 'making three shelters, one each for Jesus, Moses and Elijah'. St Luke adds, 'He spoke without knowing what he was saying'; and St Mark, 'He did not know what to say, they were so terrified'. They are totally at a loss. Certainly, the humility is there: it is all tied up with the disciples' fear.

Again, the cynic might regard the Transfiguration as nothing more than a dream. St Luke writes, 'Peter and his companions had been overcome by sleep, and when they woke they saw his glory . . .'. But the Transfiguration is very much more than just a continuation of the men's dreams. God clearly and in a powerful way made them aware of Christ in their midst . . . Moses and Elijah appearing with him, representing the Law and the Prophets of the Old Testament, emphasised that Jesus Christ is the watershed of history, who makes all the difference to things.

For the disciples, becoming really aware of Jesus Christ, as in all these miracles, means totally changing their understanding of life. The whole point of their experience is to strengthen their faith and give them a springboard for action, for coping with the difficult days ahead. Soon would come the Passion, with the big question marks it would put over their faith, and the testing of their discipleship; and later the many trials they were to experience as they set out to live Christ's way and commend it to an often hostile and ridiculing world. The Transfiguration is a 'mountain top' experience. It is during the withdrawal of the Lord with three of his disciples to pray on a mountain, in the quiet away from the crowds, the noise and the activity, that the Transfiguration happens. That is symbolical of being on the spiritual heights, just as in the Old Testament, when great times of awareness of the wonder and majesty of God are associated with mountains such as Sinai and Sion. Yet afterwards it is necessary to come down from the mountain onto the plain – to the plain of the practical, the physical, the routine and the mundane.

The main message of the Transfiguration is essentially about the Glory of Christ. He is at the centre of the whole experience. Becoming aware of his glory is something that overwhelms the disciples and initially fills them with fear. Most of all, it leads them to adore him. That awareness needs to remain with them through the very difficult days ahead. It is encapsulated so vividly in St John's account of the hours leading up to the arrest and trial of Jesus: just as Judas has gone out of the room to set in motion the events leading to the betrayal and the arrest, and ultimately the Crucifixion, the Lord says poignantly, 'Now is the Son of Man glorified' (John 13, v. 31). In the midst of all that horror and human failure – the squalid betrayal and denial, the fixed trial, the ugly, painful execution by crucifixion that seemed to underline his weakness and the triumph of the world's power – in the midst of all that, he is *glorified*! The Transfiguration isn't mentioned in St John's Gospel but its message of the glory of God in Christ is powerfully there all the time, as the central theme of the Gospel.

So what do these incidents say to us in the situations we experience and the horrors we read about in the newspapers or hear of on the TV and radio news, the fears that at times overwhelm us? Are they relevant at all? We tend to think our late twentieth century experience is very far removed from that of the select group of men in the company of Jesus Christ in a much less complicated society. Actually, our situation isn't all that different.

First of all, there is the weakness we feel about so many things in a society that can produce the most complex computer systems and explore outer space, but cannot find a way of living together in peace or conquering major killer diseases. There's the fact that so often in life there seems to be no way through something. We just hear about the latest tragedy in which lives have been ruined, and lament it, thinking, 'What can we do?' Very often, there's nothing adequate we *can* do – except bring it to the Lord in prayer.

Sometimes of course, there are small practical things. I remember vividly when, years ago, we were called back suddenly from holiday because the Rectory had been burgled. Then, it was the small practical things that helped us to cope – the church member who volunteered to take the girls to her house and kept them occupied while my wife Mary and I got ourselves sorted out; and the others who set to helping to get the mess cleared up and washing all the cutlery that had been interfered with. Then there were those who immediately rallied round when I was rushed into hospital, providing transport so that Mary could visit me in distant hospitals, and would have company on the journey at a very stressful time. Many people, I am sure, have similar stories. In those situations, it isn't just the practical help that supports us; it's the fact that people care enough to provide it without being asked.

But at the end of the day, we do feel powerless in so many situations, whether far away or close at hand. Those who find themselves ministering in a tragic situation following a massacre by a lunatic gunman or a bombing outrage or a large scale disaster are often at a loss for words. What do you say in that kind of situation? Often, there isn't a great deal to be said. And that's so often true of all bereavement care. What matters is not so much what we say, but the fact that we are there, in Christ's name, to share in loss and grief. That's what the Gospel is saying so often; it's the fact that Christ is *there* that makes all the difference.

Of course, we can never understand why miracles happen in some cases and not in others. The important thing is that Jesus Christ is there in every situation, sharing the pain, giving totally of himself. The Passion says that: and the glory of the Transfiguration leads on to the glory of the Passion; they cannot be separated. There is an anonymous story of a man dreaming and picturing his life set out over a sea shore, with two sets of footprints in the sand. They are his own and those of the Lord, representing the fact that the Lord travelled with him through all the joys and sorrows. He sees that there were times when there was only one set of footprints; and he is perturbed to notice that those were the times of the greatest distress and difficulty. He asks the Lord about this, concerned that God might have abandoned him when he needed him most; to which the Lord replies, 'My son, do you not realise that those were times when I carried you?' Faith tells us that the Lord never leaves us – least of all in our most vulnerable times. I *know* from personal experience that that is true.

V

THE LORD OF LIFE
Miracles of Resurrection

'Jesus said, "I am the resurrection and the life. Whoever has faith in me shall live, even though he die; and no-one who lives and has faith in me shall ever die"'
(John 11, v. 25)

All the miracles we have been looking at touch on some important area of human need, something vital and central to life. They have included healing and wholeness; food and drink; livelihood and the ability to earn a living; the powerfulness of the natural elements, and coping with them; spiritual awareness of God, and the meaning and purpose of life. The one thing in life that is a certain factor is its temporariness. From time to time, we hear of weird dreams of scientifically perpetuating life as we know it indefinitely; but we don't take them seriously, and it is doubtful whether many of us would greatly welcome the prospect anyway! Death is a reality that we, and our loved ones, all ultimately have to face. Thus, in a way, the Gospel miracles that involve raising from the dead are the most poignant of all, because they stand most contrary to all human experience, and because they speak to the greatest of all human concerns.

Resurrection then, is the climax of our reflection on miracles. That is certainly how the Gospels show things. There aren't many miracles that Jesus performs which involve the raising of the dead. This is the pinnacle of miracles, the one thing that in ordinary human experience doesn't happen, the miracle that causes the greatest amazement. There is the Raising of Lazarus (John 11), the Raising of the Widow's son at Nain (Luke 7) and the Raising of Jairus's daughter (Mark 5, Matthew 9 and Luke 8). We will look at those in a moment. Then of course there is the Resurrection of Jesus Christ himself. The Gospels all build up to that triumphant final note of the Resurrection; and in St John's Gospel, it is seen as the greatest miracle of all; the greatest sign of the Lord's glory. For Christians, it is the watershed of everything.

Those three incidents when Jesus raises people from the dead are in some ways preparatory events, looking forward to the Resurrection. They show that even life and death are in his hands.

The Raising of Lazarus is in John 11 . . .

> Mary came to the place where Jesus was, and as soon as she saw him she fell at his feet and said, 'Lord, if you had been here, my brother would not have died'. When Jesus saw her weeping, and the Jews who had come with her weeping, he was moved with indignation and deeply distressed. 'Where have you laid him?', he asked. They replied, 'Come and see'. Jesus wept. The Jews said, 'How dearly he must have loved him!' But some said, 'Could not this man, who opened the blind man's eyes, have done something to keep Lazarus from dying?' Jesus, again deeply moved, went to the tomb. It was a cave, with a stone placed against it. Jesus said, 'Take away the stone'. Martha, the dead man's sister, said to him, 'Sir, by now

Signs of His Glory

> there will be a stench; he has been there four days'. Jesus said, 'Did I not tell you that if you have faith you will see the glory of God?' Then they removed the stone. Jesus looked upward and said, 'Father, I thank you for hearing me. I know that you always hear me, but I have spoken for the sake of the people standing round, that they may believe that it was you who sent me.' Then he raised his voice in a great cry: 'Lazarus, come out.' The dead man came out, his hands and feet wrapped in a cloth. Jesus said, 'Loose him; let him go'. John 11, vv. 32–43)

This amazing turn around, when the man had already been buried four days, is echoed in another incident in Luke 7, where a man's funeral is taking place. He is a widow's only son; and Jesus approaches the bier and raises the dead man, to the delight and amazement of his mother and the mourners. It is the Raising of the Widow's Son at Nain.

> Afterwards, Jesus went to a town called Nain, accompanied by his disciples and a large crowd. As he approached the gate of the town, he met a funeral. The dead man was the only son of his widowed mother; and many of the townspeople were there with her. When the Lord saw her, his heart went out to her, and he said, 'Do not weep'. He stepped forward and laid his hands on the bier; and the bearers halted. Then he spoke, 'Young man, I tell you, get up'. The dead man sat up and began to speak; and Jesus restored him to his mother. Everyone was filled with awe and praised God. 'A great prophet has risen among us', they said; 'God has shown his care for his people.' The story of what he had done spread through the whole of Judea and all the region around. (Luke 7, vv. 11–17)

The Raising of Jairus's Daughter is recorded in three different Gospels (Mark 5, vv. 35–43, Matthew 9, vv. 18–26 and Luke 8, vv. 40–56). In this incident, Jesus arrives on the scene earlier than in the other two – just after the girl has died. In fact, the request for help has come to him while the girl is still alive.

He is on his way there, delayed on the journey by the woman with haemorrhage who touches his robe in the crowd to obtain a cure, when he receives the message that she has died. Again, an amazing, quite unexpected thing happens . . .

> While he was yet speaking a messenger came from the president's house, 'Your daughter has died; why trouble the teacher any more?' But Jesus, overhearing the message as it was delivered, said to the president of the synagogue, 'Do not be afraid; simply have faith'. Then he allowed no-one to accompany him except Peter and James and James's brother John. They came to the president's house, where he found a great commotion, with loud crying and wailing. So he went in and said to them, 'Why this crying and commotion? The child is not dead; she is asleep'; but they laughed at him. After turning everyone out, he took the child's father and mother and his companions into the room where the child was. Taking hold of her hand, he said to her, 'Talitha cum', which means, 'Get up, my child'. Immediately the girl got up and walked about – she was twelve years old. They were overcome with amazement . . . and he told them to give her something to eat.
> (Mark 5, vv. 35–43)

Those six strands we have found in all the Gospel miracles run through these three incidents as well: the weakness and helplessness, the humility, the amazing difference brought to things by the involvement of Christ, the need for faith and the action required of people, and most of all, the demonstration of the glory of God in Christ.

First, there is that sense of the fragility of life – the helplessness of people in the face of death. We see the sisters of Lazarus, Mary and Martha, even Jesus himself as a close friend, distraught with grief, and the friends and neighbours sharing in the family bereavement. Mary and Martha in turn both remark, 'Lord, if you had been here, my brother would

Signs of His Glory

not have died'. But it is too late – or so it seems. Lazarus has already been buried. With the widow's son at Nain, it has almost got that far; the funeral cortege is on its way for the burial. Again we are told that there are many friends and neighbours sharing in the widowed mother's sense of helplessness: 'Many of the townspeople were there with her'. In the incident concerning Jairus's daughter, Jairus is a man of some standing in the community; he is president of the synagogue. That makes no difference: his bereavement and helplessness are as great as anyone else's in similar circumstances. When the Lord arrives at Jairus's house, there is 'a great commotion, with loud crying and wailing'. In these accounts, we see bereaved sisters, bereaved parents, bereaved friends and neighbours, all quite helpless in the face of the fragility of life and the reality of death.

Then there is humility. There is perhaps an implication in the comments made by Martha and Mary of a kind of rebuke, that Jesus ought to have been there earlier to heal the sick man; but there is throughout these passages no sense of demanding or expectation of a right, but simply a putting of the situation into the Lord's hands. Jairus does not trade on his devoutness and his position as president of the synagogue; Martha and Mary do not trade on the family's friendship with Jesus; the widow at Nain doesn't ask for anything at all – it is the Lord himself who takes the initiative.

Again, in all three incidents, Jesus Christ is central to everything. In all three cases they have given up: Lazarus has been buried; the widow's son is being taken for burial; the people who have come from Jairus's house now think it's a waste of time the Lord going there ('Your daughter has died, why trouble the teacher any more?'). Against all the expectation, Jesus acts in an amazing way in each case.

Clearly in these situations, there are huge challenges to

faith, and action is required: faith going against the grain of all rational expectation, and quite ridiculous action. At the raising of Lazarus, they at first object to the notion of opening the sepulchre. Martha, ever the practical one, says in a very down to earth way, 'By now there will be a stench; he has been there four days'. Just the same, they comply; and the stone is removed. Faith in action! At Jairus's house, when Jesus says that the girl is not dead but just asleep, they laugh at him. The notion seems quite ridiculous; they have seen with their own eyes that she is dead. Amazing faith and action are required each time. And in each case, the person raised moves straight into action: Lazarus is released to walk away; the widow's son sits up speaking and is restored to his mother; Jairus's daughter gets up and walks.

All three incidents demonstrate the glory of Christ. Of the raising of Lazarus, St John writes, 'Many of the Jews who had come to see Mary and Martha, and had seen what Jesus did, put their faith in him'. Of the raising of the widow's son, St Luke writes, 'They glorified God' and 'This report went forth concerning him throughout the whole of Judea and the region round about'. Of the raising of Jairus's daughter, St Mark and St Luke both speak of people's 'amazement', and St Matthew says, 'The story became the talk of the whole district'.

There always remains the question, 'Why were *these* people raised from the dead, and not others?' It's a question that will always arise when miracles happen: 'Why?' Even more poignantly and insistently we ask in other situations: 'Why not?' We never know the answer to that question, however much we agonise over it in some dreadful situation of carnage, sudden death or terminal illness. In those situations, we just have to place ourselves in the Lord's hands, or place ourselves alongside the bereaved and the suffering, as He does in his Passion. In these three incidents, the most

Signs of His Glory

important thing of all is the fact that Jesus is *there*, that he identifies with Mary and Martha, with the widow at Nain and with Jairus and his family, and shares in their grief.

Of course, even these miracles of the raising of the dead are over-shadowed by *the* miracle – the Resurrection of Jesus Christ himself. The Resurrection of Jesus is the climax of the miracles in St John's Gospel, the greatest of all the signs of his glory, and for that matter, the triumphant miraculous note of all the Gospels. In our time, Christians have been described as *The Easter People* because the Resurrection is central to the whole Christian teaching and way of life. As St Paul writes 'If Christ was not raised, then our Gospel is null and void, and so too is your faith'. (1 Cor. 15, v. 14)

For the Resurrection, the Easter event, the Easter truth, is a miracle, in the proper sense of the word. It is a sign of the powerful transforming effect of the action of God in a totally unexpected way. This is so in two senses: in the historical event of the raising of Jesus Christ on the third day, and in the amazing transformation that came over the Lord's followers as a result of it.

None of the evangelists records the actual raising of Jesus; but there are several accounts of people's experience of the effects: the empty tomb, the various meetings that disciples had with the Risen Christ, and so on. It is possible that those accounts recorded in the Gospels are only a selection of the many experiences people had. In the account in John 20 of the discovery of the empty tomb and some of the events that followed, there is an excitement and a sense of wonder.

> Early on the first day of the week, while it was still dark, Mary of Magdala came to the tomb. She saw the stone had been moved away from the entrance, and ran to Simon Peter, and the other disciple, the one whom Jesus loved. 'They have taken the Lord out of his tomb', she said, 'and we do not know where

Signs of His Glory

they have laid him.' So Peter and the other disciple set out and made their way to the tomb. They ran together, but the other disciple ran faster than Peter and reached the tomb first. He peered in and saw the linen wrappings lying there, but did not enter. Then Simon Peter caught up with him and went into the tomb. He saw the linen wrappings lying there, and the napkin which had been round his head, not with the wrappings, but rolled up in a place by itself. Then the disciple who had reached the tomb first also went in, and he saw and believed; until then, they had not understood the Scriptures, which showed that he must rise from the dead. So the disciples went home again; but Mary stood outside the tomb weeping. And as she wept, she peered into the tomb, and she saw two angels in white sitting there, one at the head and one at the feet, where the body of Jesus had lain. They asked her, 'Why are you weeping?' She answered, 'They have taken the Lord away, and I do not know where they have laid him'. With these words, she turned round and saw Jesus standing there, but she did not recognise him. Jesus asked her, 'Why are you weeping? Who are you looking for?' Thinking it was the gardener, she said, 'If it is you, sir, who removed him, tell me where you have laid him, and I will take him away.' Jesus said, 'Mary!' She turned and said to him, 'Rabbuni!' (which is Hebrew for 'Teacher') ... Mary of Magdala went to tell the disciples ... Late that same day, the first day of the week, when the disciples were together behind locked doors for fear of the Jews, Jesus came and stood among them. 'Peace be with you!', he said; then he showed them his hands and his side. On seeing the Lord, the disciples were overjoyed. Jesus said again, 'Peace be with you!' ... One of the Twelve, Thomas the Twin, was not with the rest when Jesus came. So the others kept telling him, 'We have seen the Lord.' But he said, 'Unless I see the mark of the nails on his hands, unless I put my finger into the place where the nails were, and my hand into his side, I will never believe it.' A week later, his disciples were once again in the

Signs of His Glory

> room, and Thomas was with them. Although the doors were locked, Jesus came and stood among them, saying, 'Peace be with you!' Then he said to Thomas, 'Reach your finger here; look at my hands. Reach your hand here and put it into my side. Be unbelieving no longer, but believe.' Thomas said, 'My Lord and my God!' Jesus said to him, 'Because you have seen me you have found faith. Happy are they who find faith without seeing me.' There were indeed many other signs that Jesus performed in the presence of his disciples, which are not recorded in this book. (John 20, vv. 1–30)

Of course none of that fits in with the material world as we know it; the whole thing is so extraordinary, so amazing. Many people have tried to explain it all away, or have made cynical remarks about 'conjuring tricks with bones', and so on. It has been suggested that Jesus wasn't really dead when his body was taken down from the cross, and that he was revived later. That is nonsense when you read the details of the accounts of the Crucifixion and the Burial. It has even been suggested that the meetings with the Risen Christ were invented by the writers of the Gospels, or were part of the folklore that grew up after the event. That is a quite extraordinary suggestion. It is quite clear that the disciples were not really expecting it to happen (despite the teaching Jesus had given them), and at first sight didn't believe it; and that they were happy for that initial lack of faith to be included in the accounts. The way the disciples are portrayed in these accounts has the ring of truth about it. It should be remembered too, what preaching the Resurrection brought them in the way of persecution, and that in most cases, it ultimately brought them martyrdom. There was little motive for inventing it all. At the end of the day, it is a much more tortuous exercise explaining the Resurrection away than it is trying to understand and explain it.

Signs of His Glory

In fact, Christians don't need to get all twisted up in apologetics for the Resurrection; we simply know it to be true. It's at the heart of what the Gospel is about. Because Jesus Christ is risen, we can know him in the Eucharist, and we can be certain that he walks beside us through life. As I wrote in an earlier chapter, that was something I was made vividly aware of during my weeks of hospitalisation and intensive treatment. Somehow, I just knew increasingly that the Easter message was true, that the Risen Christ was with me in a powerful way, however things developed; and that experience has transformed my spiritual life. Countless experiences of Christians through the centuries would underline the same thing. St Paul, in his first Letter to the Christians at Corinth, sees a natural progression from what happened to the Christians at the first Easter, to our own hope: because *he* is risen, *we* are risen. That of course affects the whole Christian understanding of and approach to life and death. The Resurrection of Jesus Christ is the watershed of history.

Of course, we don't fully grasp what the Resurrection actually involved. Clearly the Risen Lord was not just a resuscitated revived Jesus of Nazareth; nor was he just a spirit or a ghost. To start with he was not recognised even by those who knew him best – Mary Magdalene, at first thought he was the gardener, and the disciples on the road to Emmaus did not know him until the Breaking of Bread. The way that Jesus was suddenly there and suddenly gone; the way that doors and walls were no barrier to him, but he ate with and conversed with the disciples: all these things say that he was different. As St John's Gospel often puts it, he was glorified. No wonder St John sees the Resurrection as the climax of miracles, to which the whole Gospel builds up, the greatest of all the signs of the Lord's glory.

Signs of His Glory

There is another sense in which the Resurrection is the climax of miracles. There is what happened to that little inner group of the followers of Jesus, the Apostles. The way they were totally transformed is quite amazing, quite extraordinary. During the events of the Passion, and then at the time when they encountered the Risen Christ, they were men of doubt, not knowing what was going to happen next. They were filled with terror, so that they ran away when the Lord was arrested; and they were behind closed doors, 'for fear of the Jews' when the Risen Lord came to them. They were depressed and overcome with the horror and seeming hopelessness of things, so that in the Garden of Gethsemane they slept, 'worn out with grief'. Yet later, after the experience of meeting with and knowing the Risen Christ, the Apostles were certain, as they preached 'Jesus and the Resurrection'. Fear changed to courage and bewilderment changed to certainty. In the face of all kinds of setbacks, afflictions and ridicules, they went out with the Resurrection message; and they were overjoyed, even in the face of pain and imprisonment, and ultimately martyrdom. They changed dramatically; indeed, in a sense, *they* had died and risen. That is all part of the miracle of the Resurrection. And again, we can see those six strands that we have found in all the Gospel miracles.

First, there is the weakness, the fragility, the helplessness. That comes through very clearly in the hours and days following the Crucifixion: that sense of total helplessness and lack of direction, like a boat that has lost its rudder, and is meandering aimlessly around. It is as if the disciples are waiting for something to happen, but they don't exactly know what, despite all the quite explicit teaching Jesus has given them. The true significance of it all only comes to them afterwards.

There is certainly humility involved in it too. There can hardly be anything else, after what has happened. The disciples are acutely aware of how they have failed him by misunderstanding, by running away – even, in St Peter's case, by denying, under interrogation, that he ever knew him. Gathered in the room behind locked doors, or rushing to the garden to examine the empty tomb, they would have an overwhelming sense of their own failings and inadequacy.

It all centres, as it must, on Jesus Christ. That stands to reason. After the Crucifixion, it is the fact that the Lord has been taken away from them that is the most stunning thing. When Mary Magdalene goes to the garden, it is to tend the body of Jesus; and when she discovers the empty tomb and then meets Jesus and thinks he is the gardener, she complains, 'They have taken my Lord away, and I do not know where they have laid him'. His Resurrection changes everything: the evangelist remarks, 'Then were they overjoyed when they saw the Lord'.

Then there is faith. To start with, the disciples are woefully lacking in faith; and who can blame them? When Mary Magdalene meets Jesus in the garden and mistakes him for the gardener, it is partly because he is different that she does not at first recognise him; but it is also because she does not expect to meet him. She is only expecting that someone has moved the Lord's body that she has come to anoint. No doubt Peter and John too, running to the tomb, fear the same kind of desecration. Then later on, Thomas will not believe the others. It is meeting the Risen Christ that lifts them out of that doubt to a new rock-solid faith – a faith which will be greatly tested through the years of persecution, and which will come through triumphant.

This ties up with the action that was required of the disciples. It was the Pentecost experience that fired and empowered them with the Spirit of God, making incredible things possible; but it all began with the Resurrection. The amazing thing is the speed with which the Resurrection faith spread far and wide, as that little group of disciples acted as his messengers, in ways they wouldn't have dreamt possible.

All that redounds to the Glory of God; that is what it's all about. Miracles happen in the way people are changed by God's hand.

In a way, that is always true. It is not just a question of sudden conversion – although that does happen of course; people do have 'Damascus road' experiences. Nevertheless conversion is more often than not an ongoing lifelong experience. I remember many years ago going to answer the Vicarage doorbell, to be met with the opening question, 'Have you been converted?' What a question to be confronted with on a vicarage doorstep! However, the questioners were not travelling evangelists; they were two men in green overalls who wanted to know whether our gas supply had been converted to natural gas! In due course, the conversion was completed; but there were teething problems, and we had engineers constantly coming back to restart the central heating. The neighbours told us too that their gas cookers took quite some time before they were working properly! That seemed to me a vivid parable about conversion. Things don't just happen in a flash. Christian discipleship is a constant experience of death and resurrection, as God gives us fresh starts and does amazing things with us. That is often miraculous, in the true sense of the word.

And we need all those strands: awareness of our weak fragility; humility; Christ at the centre of it all; faith against all the odds; readiness to do things in faith, often things that go against the grain and seem quite crazy, quite impossible. Above all we need the recognition that, at the end of the day,

God is Lord, Jesus is Lord, and will ultimately triumph, whatever the problems, because he is the Lord of Life – eternal life.

Canon Ronald Lunt was born in 1930, and after training at Ely Theological College, was ordained in 1958, serving his entire ministry in the Diocese of Chester. From 1978 to 1996, he was Rector of Chester, and for most of that time Rural Dean of Chester. He was a member of the General Synod of the Church of England until 1995. This book is a reflection on the Gospel miracles against the background of his personal experience of suddenly having to come to terms with serious illness and discovering afresh the power of prayer and renewal of faith.